FIGHTER PILOTS

> ## What It Takes to Join the Elite

TIM RIPLEY

Cavendish
Square
New York

Published in 2016 by Cavendish Square Publishing, LLC
243 5th Avenue, Suite 136, New York, NY 10016

© 2016 Brown Bear Books Ltd

First Edition

Website: cavendishsq.com

This publication represents the opinions and views of the author based on his or her personal experiences, knowledge, and research. The information in this book serves as a general guide only. the author and publisher have used their best efforts in preparing this book and disclaim liability rising directly or indirectly from the use and application of this book.

CPSIA Compliance Information: Batch #WS15CSQ

Library of Congress Cataloging-in-Publication Data

Ripley, Tim.
  Fighter pilots : what it takes to join the elite / Tim Ripley.
     pages cm. — (Military jobs)
  Includes bibliographical references and index.
  ISBN 978-1-50260-512-2 (hardcover) ISBN 978-1-50260-513-9 (ebook)
  1. Fighter pilots—Training of—United States. 2. Fighter plane combat—United States.
  3. Fighter pilots—Vocational guidance—United States. I. Title.

  UG638.R57 2016
  358.4'302373—dc23

                         2014049216

For Brown Bear Books Ltd:
Editorial Director: Lindsey Lowe
Managing Editor: Tim Cooke
Children's Publisher: Anne O'Daly
Design Manager: Keith Davis
Designer: Lynne Lennon
Picture Manager: Sophie Mortimer

Picture Credits:
T=Top, C=Center, B=Bottom, L=Left, R=Right

Front Cover: U.S. Department of Defense
All images U.S. Department of Defense except: U.S. National Archives 7.
Artistic Effects: Shutterstock

Manufactured in the United States of America

CONTENTS

INTRODUCTION

Hurtling through the air at faster than the speed of sound in one of the most powerfully armed fighting machines in the world, fighter pilots need lightning reflexes, steady nerves, and reliable judgment.

Fighter pilots are among the most highly qualified members of the US Air Force. Modern war jets cost around $100 million each, so only the best pilots in the service get the chance to fly them.

The process of becoming a jet pilot is demanding, Even to begin pilot training, candidates have to graduate as Air Force officers. The men and women who undertake pilot training need dedication, physical fitness, and academic smarts. They are usually in the top three percent of their high school class. There is huge competition for places—only one in every nine applicants gets on to the course. Every candidate needs to be nominated by a member of Congress. They must also be unmarried and have no dependents, because they will be traveling widely and will spend much of their time away from home.

 Major Shawna Kimbrell, the Air Force's first female black pilot, poses with her F-16 Fighting Falcon.

HISTORY

The Wright Brothers made the first powered flight in 1903. Just over a decade later, warplanes made their first appearance. Since then, fighter planes have featured in every major conflict across the world.

The first fighter planes flew in World War I (1914–1918). To begin with, they were used to observe the enemy lines beneath. Soon, however, the pilots started shooting at each other with pistols. Later, the aircraft were fitted with machine guns.

World War II

In World War II (1939–1945), fighters became quicker and more powerful. Their main task was to protect bombers from enemy fighters. The German Messerschmitt Me 262 was the first fighter powered by a jet turbine. Although it was quicker than other aircraft, the Me 262 was a subsonic airplane, so it flew slower than the speed of sound.

Lieutenant Colonel Richard F. Turner climbs out of the cockpit of his F-100 Super Sabre after a mission during the Korean War.

Jet Power

The first jet fighters to fly quicker than the speed of sound (767 miles per hour; 1,235 kmh) appeared in the early 1950s. The US F-100 Super Sabre fought against Soviet MiG jets in the Korean War (1950–1953) and again during the conflict in Vietnam (1961–1975).

Today, all fighters are jets. Their pilots are some of the most highly trained of all combatants. They can fly deep into enemy territory to strike at ground targets.

 Black pilots of the 332nd Fighter Group—the Tuskegee Airmen— discuss a mission during World War II.

IN ACTION

In World War I, pilots who shot down five or more enemy aircraft became known as aces. The name stuck. The top US ace of World War I was Eddie Rickenbacker, with twenty-six "kills." In World War II, Richard I. Bong shot down at least forty Japanese aircraft. The top US ace of the Korean War was Joseph C. McConnell, with sixteen victories.

≫≫ WHAT IT TAKES

Qualifying to fly a jet fighter is a long and demanding process. Fighter pilots are the elite of the US Air Force. They have to be physically fit and mentally sharp, with nerves of steel.

The first stage in the process is to qualify for Officer Training School. All applicants must hold a bachelor's degree and be between the ages of eighteen and thirty-four. They must also pass the Air Force Officer Qualifying Test. This five-hour exam tests their reasoning skills and also their ability

 A training instructor gives orders to a new recruit at Officer Training School.

New graduates parade at Maxwell Air Force Base, Alabama, after successfully completing Air Force Officer Training School.

to read aviation instruments and judge speed. Applicants must also pass a series of health checks, including having good eyesight.

Officer Training School

A selection board decides who is admitted to Officer Training School. The twelve-week course includes studying military strategy and history. While studying, candidates also exercise every day to get their bodies into peak condition. They also learn about the Air Force's principles of conduct and leadership.

IN ACTION

Since 1993, both men and women have been eligible to train as fighter pilots, but female pilots remain a relative minority. Of the 3,700 fighter pilots in the US Air Force, only about seventy are female. That still represents a higher ratio of female pilots than in many other air forces around the world, however.

PILOT SELECTION

Getting to fly some of the quickest and deadliest machines in the world is not easy. Only outstanding candidates ever reach a fighter cockpit.

 An airman crosses a rope on an obstacle course during physical training. All pilots are expected to have high fitness levels.

Becoming a fighter pilot requires a serious commitment. Because the training is so long and expensive, Air Force pilots must agree to spend at least ten years on active duty.

Pilots wearing life preservers are briefed before a water survival exercise.

Potential pilots graduate as officers from the Maxwell Air Force Base in Alabama, the Air Force Reserve Officer Training Corps, or an Air Force Officer Training School. They then undergo selection for pilot training. This checks not just a candidate's aptitude for flying, but also his or her suitability for military life.

Physical Demands

Flying a jet is physically demanding. Pilots experience huge amounts of "G force," when acceleration multiplies the effects of gravity on the body. Pilots have to be physically fit to ensure that they do not throw up or pass out under such physical stress.

EYEWITNESS

"It's a bit more extensive than the average college admissions process. This became clear when I asked the kid next to me at freshman orientation what he got on the SATs and he responded, '1600' without blinking."

—Cameron Schaefer, US Air Force pilot

FLIGHT TRAINING

Once a trainee pilot gets to fly an airplane, he or she is still months away from becoming a fighter pilot. To begin with, trainees fly basic propeller airplanes and practice in sophisticated simulators.

An Air Force lieutenant prepares for an exercise in a simulator based on the A-10 Warthog.

Potential fighter pilots begin their flight training on the T-6A Texan II turbo-prop training aircraft at bases across the southern United States. After they have

 The T-6A has a seat in back for an experienced instructor to observe the pilot's skills firsthand.

ninety hours flying time, students move on to low-level flying skills and airborne navigation. When they are not flying, students study aeronautical science, navigation, and aerospace engineering.

The Sound Barrier

Successful students move on to the T-38C Talon II. In this Vietnam War-era jet, they break the sound barrier for the first time, reaching speeds of Mach 1.3. Over 120 hours of flying, they practice air-to-air combat, low-level ground attack missions,

and formation flying. Finally, those candidates who make the grade are awarded the famous silver wings of a US Air Force pilot—the mark of an elite military aviator.

EYEWITNESS

"You're going up against a lot of guys who are used to succeeding in life, lots of type-A personalities. There are a limited number of pilot slots and so you're graded on everything you do then racked and stacked at the end."

—Cameron Schaefer, US Air Force pilot

▶▶ FAST JET TRAINING

If they get through flight training, graduates are entitled to wear the coveted pilot's wings on their uniforms. However, the training does not stop.

The new pilots are posted to learn how to fly the Air Force's frontline combat jets, like the F-22 Raptor and the F-15E Strike Eagle. Different bases specialize in different models of fighter. Each has its own "schoolhouse" where pilots learn about the technical and engineering details of their new aircraft, as well as the highly sophisticated smart weapons and electronic sensors they carry into combat.

The two-seat T-38 Talon is a high-altitude, supersonic jet used for advanced training.

VN
25 FTS

U.S. AIR FORCE

VN

Intense Training

The combat training includes dog-fighting, ground-attack missions, and air support for combat search-and-rescue missions. This involves live strafing runs with cannons, firing air-to-air missiles, and dropping laser-guided bombs.

At the end of this intense training, pilots are ready to go into action. They are posted to units across the world, whether it be standing alert to protect America's cities, helping defend allies in Europe and Asia, or in combat in the Middle East.

 A current pilot and a former US Air Force instructor pilot land in a specially painted T-38 to celebrate the airplane's fiftieth anniversary in 2011.

IN ACTION

The initial phase of flight training is completed by all US Air Force pilots. At its conclusion, pilots decide on a specialty. As well as those who go on to fly fighter jets, others fly bombers, "heavy lift" transport and refueling aircraft, or helicopters. They train for their chosen discipline.

►► CARRIER LANDING TRAINING

The US Navy and Marine Corps have their own training programs to prepare pilots to fly from aircraft carriers at sea.

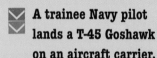 **A trainee Navy pilot lands a T-45 Goshawk on an aircraft carrier.**

Taking off from and landing on a moving ship at sea requires an even greater level of skill than flying from land bases. Navy and Marine Corps pilots share similar basic training to the Air Force. They fly the

T-6A Texan to build up their flying skills. However, they also learn tailhook training, which prepares them to land on the deck of an aircraft carrier, even in stormy weather at night.

Landing at Sea

Pilots practice in T-45 Goshawk jets. They use a simulated aircraft-carrier deck on an airfield runway fitted with an arrester hook. The hook brings the airplane to a sudden halt when it lands. The trainees then move on to landing on and taking off from a Nimitz class aircraft carrier.

Successful naval and marine aviators are awarded their gold wings. They go on to learn how to fly the Hornet strike jet or Harrier jump jet in combat.

IN ACTION

A crucial phase in learning to land on a carrier is to learn what to do when things go wrong. All pilots learn to escape from a submerged aircraft. They train in swimming pools in special pods that can replicate any position of an aircraft underwater. The focus is on training recruits so they do not panic if their aircraft hits the water.

A pilot is submerged upside down in a pool as he practices escaping from a downed airplane.

►►► EXERCISE RED FLAG

Fighter pilots constantly improve their skills. Several times a year, the US Air Force holds Exercise Red Flag high above the Nevada Desert.

Hundreds of fighters and bombers, together with reconnaissance, air-to-air refueling, and command aircraft, fly together in simulated air wars.

▽ **A flight of F-15 Eagles and F-16 Fighting Falcons prepares for the exercise.**

High above the Nevada Desert, Aggressor aircraft seek their "enemies."

Simulated Combat

For a month at a time, pilots and aircrew fly daily missions that simulate real air-to-air or air-to-ground combat. Satellite and laser devices replicate the performance of live weapons, allowing crews to claim realistic "kills" or to be "killed" themselves.

Red Flag is the nearest thing to real combat most pilots ever face. An elite "enemy" squadron, known as the Aggressors, challenges the "blue" or "friendly" forces. The Aggressors are the best pilots in the US military, so they push their

"enemies" to the limit. The only difference from real combat is that at Red Flag a mistake is not fatal.

EYEWITNESS

"This exercise is important because it gives our pilots, along with pilots of our NATO allies, the opportunity to train under simulated combat conditions. This helps to prepare them for almost anything they might encounter in an actual combat zone."

—Erick Martinez, airman

AIR SUPREMACY

The main mission of a fighter pilot is to gain air supremacy by clearing the skies of enemy aircraft, removing any threat to friendly forces from the air.

Pilots need to locate enemy aircraft and then either shoot them down or chase them away. They do this by using a combination of long-range missiles, powerful radar, and stealth technology.

A flight of F/A-18 Hornets flies in a column formation high above Louisiana on an exercise.

Out of Range

US Air Force fighters are all equipped with radar-guided Advanced Medium-Range Air-to-Air Missiles (AMRAAM). They can hit enemy aircraft over 50 miles (80 km) away. This range usually allows US pilots to stay safely out of enemy range. It also means they can always get the first shot in against any opponent, which is a key advantage in any aerial duel.

 Carrier-based aircraft fly in formation over the Pacific as part of a demonstration of air power.

If enemy aircraft manage to get past the AMRAAMs, US pilots have heat-seeking Sidewinder missiles for closer range combat. They lock on to the hot exhaust of any enemy jet.

Patrolling the Skies

Once enemy fighters are cleared, pilots remain on patrol to prevent them returning. Around-the-clock combat air patrols over enemy air bases help to keep hostile aircraft on the ground. The stealth protection of the F-22 Raptor makes it ideal for this task. It does not reflect radar signals, making it difficult for the enemy to track it effectively.

IN ACTION

The advanced long- and medium-range missiles in the US armory give pilots a real advantage. They can engage most enemies without having to fly within range of the enemy's own weapons.

AIR-TO-GROUND OPERATIONS

Although many attacks on ground targets are carried out by bombers, fighter pilots are called upon to use the speed and advanced weaponry of their jet planes to make raids on targets behind enemy lines.

Fighter pilots have a range of machine guns, missiles, and bombs to hit targets with pinpoint accuracy—but they have to get to the target first. On missions deep into enemy territory, pilots use electronic jamming to disable enemy radar. Pilots also use flares and other countermeasures that "confuse" enemy weapons.

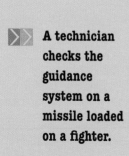 **A technician checks the guidance system on a missile loaded on a fighter.**

These methods help pilots avoid enemy surface-to-air missiles defending important targets.

 An F/A-18A Hornet fires a 5-inch Zuni air-to-ground missile during an exercise.

Finding Targets

It is challenging to identify a target while flying at supersonic speeds. Pilots use target pods fitted with infrared video cameras that can identify small targets, even individuals. Pilots monitor the video feed and select targets for attack. They either download coordinates into satellite-guided bombs or point laser designators at the target to direct bombs. It is essential to avoid killing or injuring civilians. Modern weapons are also expensive, so pilots have to be sure they have the right target before pressing the weapon release control.

EYEWITNESS

"SAM [surface-to-air missile] hunting is the most dangerous mission faced by today's fighter pilots, a job more hazardous and dangerous than shooting down enemy jets."

—Dan Hampton, F-16 pilot

▷▷ COUNTER INSURGENCY

Fighter pilots are in the forefront of the U.S. response to irregular warfare against terrorists and insurgents. It requires strength of character to be the first U.S. forces to engage such an enemy.

In conflicts in Afghanistan, Iraq, and Syria, terrorists fight largely through tactics such as hit and run attacks, snipers, and improvised explosive devices (IEDs). Fighters can attack suspected enemy positions directly, or can provide cover for friendly forces on the ground.

Smoke rises from an insurgent camp after a US air strike in Afghanistan in 2011.

A cockpit camera captures an explosion during a US fighter attack on ISIL positions in Mosul, Iraq, in September 2014.

Show of Strength

Fighter pilots fly into enemy territory from bases in neighboring countries. Insurgents often shelter among the civilian population, so pilots need to have confidence in their own ability to identify a target. Once they are in position to launch a strike, they cannot afford to hesitate.

Pilots fly within range of insurgent weapons, so there is a danger of being shot down. Fighter pilots learn survival and escape techniques in case they are shot down in enemy territory.

Strikes in Syria

In September 2014, US fighter pilots struck at targets controlled by Islamic State (ISIL) rebels in Syria and Iraq. The strikes were intended to destroy insurgent fighting positions.

EYEWITNESS

"We wanted to make sure ISIL knew they had no safe haven, and we certainly achieved that."

—General Martin Dempsey, Joint Chiefs of Staff, 2014

25

PRECISION WEAPONS

Any U.S. Air Force fighter pilot has to be a weapons expert. The wide range of weaponry means that pilots have to be able to understand what weapon is best for what task. Every mission uses precision guided or "smart" weapons.

An F-16C Fighting Falcon drops a 2,000-pound (905 kg) laser-guided bomb during an exercise.

The most widely used guided weapons are Joint Direct Attack Munitions (JDAMs). They have warheads up to 2,000 pounds (905 kg) and use satellite guidance to strike within 165 feet (50 m) of their intended

 Technicians at a US Air
Force base in Iraq examine a
laser-guided bomb on an F-16
Fighting Falcon.

targets, even at night or in bad
weather. JDAMs have largely
replaced laser-guided missiles,
which had to be guided by a pilot.

Other Missiles

To hit targets deep inside enemy
territory, the US Air Force uses
the new Joint Air-to-Surface
Standoff Missile (JASSM). To
avoid collateral damage, it uses
the Small Diameter Bomb (SDB).
This can be used to hit high-value
targets that cannot be attacked
with bigger weapons.

IN ACTION

JDAMs have proved more reliable than
the former laser-guided missiles. A pilot
had to direct the missile by "painting"
the target with a laser during his
bombing run. Bad weather or enemy
fire could interfere with the laser,
causing the missile to miss its target.

⟫ CARRIER OPERATIONS

Since World War II (1939–1945), the United States has used its aircraft carriers to allow its fighter pilots to operate anywhere in the world.

An F/A-18C Hornet prepares to launch from the deck of USS *John C. Stennis.*

The Navy calls its Nimitz class nuclear-powered carriers "4.5 acres of sovereign territory." They can sail anywhere and launch their jets without the need to consult allies to gain access to air bases. The pilots of carrier-launched F/A-18 Hornet jets conduct the full range of combat operations. Their first job is fleet defense, flying combat air patrols over

their carrier battle group. They can also attack enemy warships and other vessels with guns and guided missiles.

An F/A-18 Super Hornet launches from the deck of the USS *Abraham Lincoln* in the Arabian Gulf in 2012.

Crossing the Beach

During offensive operations, the Hornets are sent "across the beach" to hit enemy targets inland using smart bombs and missiles. Hornets could soon be joined on the decks of the carriers by X-47 unmanned combat drones, which are designed with stealth features to allow them to penetrate through heavy enemy defenses.

EYEWITNESS

"To aid the landing pilot, the ship has an optical device that projects a beam of light toward the planes approaching to land. This is the glide path that I want to follow down to a safe touchdown in the middle of the arresting gear."

—Barry Hampe, former US Navy pilot

F-22 RAPTOR

Virtually every hopeful US fighter pilot sets out wanting to fly the F-22 Raptor, the most advanced fighter in the US forces. Only those who perform outstandingly in training get the choice of flying the world's hottest fighter.

The F-22 Raptor is the US Air Force's only frontline stealth fighter. Its sleek lines and two engines give it supersonic performance, while its profile and low radar signature enable it to pass unnoticed inside enemy airspace.

 Vapor trails from the wing tips of an F-22 Raptor as it speeds through the sky.

 The F-22's glass cockpit has a heads-up display and a wide field of vision for the pilot.

Air Supremacy

From bases in the United States, Pacific, and Middle East, the F-22 has been providing air supremacy since 2005. The F-22 was developed purely in order to achieve air supremacy. More recently, however, it was transformed into a bomber by modifying the weapons bays and targeting computers to allow it to carry satellite-guided Joint Direct Attack Munitions (JDAMs).

F-22 RAPTOR
Top speed: 1,500 mph (2,410 kmh)
Range: 1,840 miles (2,960 km)
Weapons: 1 x 20 mm cannon; up to 2,000 lbs (900 kg) ordnance

IN ACTION

The latest stealth features make the F-22 invisible to enemy radar, by using shapes and materials to deflect radio waves. To boost the stealth performance, all weapons are carried in internal bays. To fire a missile, the bay has to open for just one second.

F-16 FIGHTING FALCON

Most US fighter pilots fly the famous F-16 Fighting Falcon or Viper. Some 4,500 aircraft have been built in the past forty years, and the F-16 remains the mainstay of the US fighter fleet.

The F-16 is also popular with many of America's allies. Fighter pilots in more than twenty-five air forces around the world praise the aircraft as the "fighter pilot's fighter." It is highly maneuverable in dogfights, and is helped by an impressive power-to-weight ratio that gives it a dramatic rate of climb that helps it get out of any dangerous situations. Its distinctive cockpit gives its pilot a clear view of the world.

 Captain Michael Leary of 4th Fighter Squadron returns to base in his F-16 after an exercise.

Two F-16s break away after being refueled by a Stratotanker aircraft over Iraq in 2011.

Many Roles

Since the Viper entered service with the US Air Force in 1979, it has progressively improved with new weapons. Today's F-16 pilot can take on opponents with radar-guided air-to-air missiles, satellite and laser-guided bombs, and standoff cruise missiles.

Major Conflicts

US Viper pilots have fought in every major war of the past twenty-five years, spearheading the 1991 and 2003 Gulf Wars, and flying above the conflicts in Balkans, Libya, and Afghanistan.

F-16 FIGHTING FALCON
Top speed: 1,500 mph (2,414 kmh)
Range: 2,425 miles (3,900 km)
Weapons: 1 x 20 mm cannon; up to 17,000 lbs (7,700 kg) ordnance

EYEWITNESS

"I was riveted to my radar altimeter, which gave me a digital readout of my actual height above the ground. A lifesaver at night or in bad weather. Like now."

—Lt. Col. Dan Hampton, F-16 pilot, Iraq, 2005

F/A-18 HORNET

Since the retirement of the F-14 Tomcat in 2006, the Hornet has been the US Navy's only carrier-launched fighter. Navy and Marine Corps pilots have flown Hornets since the early 1980s.

The two-engined Hornet has a tailhook to allow it to land on Nimitz-class carriers. Its reinforced undercarriage can be connected to the carriers' steam catapults to be launched over the bows.

The Navy and Marines have flown several variants of the Hornet. A two-seat model flies specialized close air-support missions for the Marines. New E and F variants, dubbed the Super Hornet, are

 An F/A-18 Hornet refuels from an air tanker at sunset in the skies above Iraq.

 Two F/A-18s patrol the skies. The aircraft have a range of up to 1,250 miles (2,000 km).

in full production with enhanced engines and sensors and a wider portfolio of weapons. A dedicated electronic warfare variant, the EA-18G Growler, flies from aircraft carriers to jam enemy radar and communications.

In Action

Hornet pilots have seen action from Iraq to Afghanistan, Libya, and the Balkans. At any time, two US Navy carriers—each with fifty Hornets—are at sea, patrolling the world's trouble spots.

F/A-18 HORNET
Top speed: 1,190 mph (1,915 kmh)
Range: 1,250 miles (2,000 km)
Weapons: 1 x 20 mm cannon; up to 13,700 lbs (6,200 kg) ordnance

EYEWITNESS

"I pushed the throttles into full afterburner and the aircraft accelerated through the sound barrier, with only a gentle bump to indicate that we had gone supersonic."

—Carlo Kopp, Australian F/A-18 pilot

⯈⯈ A-10 THUNDERBOLT

Fighter pilots are often rude about the A-10 Thunderbolt. Its ugly appearance—it has twin vertical tails, big engines, and a stubby cannon—led them to rename it the Warthog. But the "hog drivers" who fly the aircraft appreciate its power.

It may look ugly, but the A-10 packs a powerful punch. It is also thickly armored, so it can take a heavy pounding. The A-10 was planned as a "tank killer," using its nose-mounted Gatling gun and Maverick missiles.

Design Features

The fighter's engines are mounted outside the fuselage, so, even if it is hit, the aircraft can still keep flying. The

⯈⯈ The external engines of the A-10 help give the unusual appearance that earned its "Warthog" nickname.

>> **The seven-barrel gatling gun in the Warthog's nose is designed to destroy enemy tanks.**

titanium-lined cockpit makes the "hog drivers" the best protected pilots in the world.

The uranium-tipped shells of the A-10's 30mm Gatling gun can rip through the armor of any tank in the world. For troops locked in combat, the distinctive sound of an approaching A-10 is a real boost to morale.

A-10 THUNDERBOLT
Top speed: 439 mph (706 kmh)
Range: 800 miles (1,290 km)
Weapons: 1 x 30 mm cannon; up to 16,000 lbs (7,260 kg) ordnance

EYEWITNESS

"You see [the A-10] come on station, you know what it's capable of. You know that the enemy on the other side probably doesn't want to mess with you while that's in the air."

—**Major Daniel O'Hara, US Marine Corps, Afghanistan**

F-35 JOINT STRIKE FIGHTER

The F-35 Lightning II is the very latest US fighter. Like the F-22 Raptor, only the most outstanding pilots will get to fly the advanced machine.

By 2020, hundreds of the new jets will be flying with the US Air Force, Navy, and Marine Corps. The F-35 shares the stealth features of the F-22, and its upgraded sensors and weapons options. Unlike the Raptor, however, the F-35 is designed mainly as a

 Lt. Col. Eric Smith of 58th Fighter Squadron, the first F-35 pilot in the Air Force, taxis his aircraft in 2011.

An F-35 soars above an airbase in Florida in 2011.

strike aircraft to hit targets deep inside enemy territory or to support troops on the battlefield.

Three Variants

There are three main variants of the aircraft. The F-35A is optimized for operations from runways. The F-35B is adapted for vertical take-off and landing (VTOL), so it can support Marine Corps units in beachheads. The F-35C is adapted for flying from aircraft carriers. That will give the Navy a manned stealth capability. The F-35 was first used in action in Syria and Iraq in 2014.

F-35 JOINT STRIKE FIGHTER
Top speed: 1,200 mph (1,930 kmh)
Range: 1, 365 miles (2,200 km)
Weapons: 1 x 25 mm cannon; up to 18,000 lbs (8,100 kg) ordnance

EYEWITNESS

"The F-35 is a digital airplane: There are no gauges, dials, or analog displays. The throttle and stick enable the pilot to fly ... both are loaded with buttons and switches to control sensors, weapons, and target selection, communications, and autopilot, among other things."

—Colonel Art Tomassetti, pilot, US Marine Corps

CLOSE AIR SUPPORT

When troops call for Close Air Support (CAS), they are often pinned down in desperate situations. Fighter pilots attack the enemy troops on the ground.

An A-10 pilot banks away as his missiles strike the ground below.

When a group of US Navy SEALs were pinned down on an Afghan mountain in March 2002 after their helicopter had

been shot down, they called up F-15E Strike Eagles to keep the enemy at bay. The pilots could hear bullets hitting around the SEALs over the radios.

In their first passes, the F-15Es unloaded their Joint Direct Attack Munuition (JDAMs) on hundreds of insurgents surrounding the SEALs. When they had run out of bombs, the F-15Es turned to their 30mm cannons and began making strafing runs. The presence of the US fighters saved the day and the SEALs were eventually rescued.

 Combat controllers watch an A-10 release its weapons during an exercise in the Nevada desert.

EYEWITNESS

"Our primary mission [close air support] is to make noise. We are up there to let the bad guys know what we're capable of and to keep them hunkered down ... The airplane overhead gives people on the ground an umbrella of safety that is basically irreplaceable."

—Lt. Col. Michael Brill, US Air Force F-16 pilot

SURVEILLANCE

Because only fighter jets can get past enemy air defenses, US fighter pilots are often the only people who can gather vital intelligence on the enemy, using sophisticated surveillance cameras.

During the Battle of Fallujah in 2004, insurgents captured the Iraqi city and fought off US and Iraqi troops. The insurgents turned the city into a fortress, with minefields, road blocks, and ambushes blocking routes into Fallujah.

Reconnaissance

US Marine Corps F/A-18 Hornet pilots were sent to photograph every inch of the city using their photographic reconnaissance pods. In order to try to catch insurgents out in the open,

An F-16 pilot uses night vision goggles to follow action on the ground in the dark.

 A still from a weapons system video of an F-16 shows the location of an airstrike that killed three insurgent leaders in Iraq in 2007. (Some secret information was covered up before the image was released.)

the Hornet pilots made high-speed low-level dashes across the city from unexpected directions. These low-level passes exposed the Hornets to ground fire. The pilots had to have nerves of steel to stay on course as machine-gun and missile fire arced up toward their jets. US Air Force F-16 Viper pilots also joined this effort using the video cameras in their targeting pods to monitor the streets.

Learning the City

Flying high over the city, the US pilots filmed daily life as the population and insurgents moved around. When US and Iraqi troops finally launched their

counterattack to reclaim the city, the ground commanders had precise information about the enemy. In addition, the pilots knew the streets of Fallujah so well that they could respond to calls for help from coalition assault troops in a matter of minutes.

IN ACTION

Close air support is usually directed by US Air Force Combat Controllers. These expert air-traffic controllers serve with troops on the ground. They locate targets and coordinate air strikes—even when the targets are close to their own positions.

►► AIR POLICING

On combat air patrol, fighter pilots keep watch for hostile actions, both near international trouble spots and above the United States itself.

 Female F-15 pilots prepare to go on patrol from an air base in Alaska in 2006.

Pilots often fly combat air patrols (CAP) above US territory in response to specific threats, such as in the days after the terrorist attacks of September 11, 2001. They intercept

aircraft that do not respond to communications, or that are heading toward a major city or sports event. Their job is to make sure such aircraft do not represent any threat.

 F-16s patrol above the Pentagon in Washington, DC, in the days after the 9/11 attacks of 2001.

Policing the Russians

In March 2014 Russia clashed with its neighbor, Ukraine. Russian aircraft made regular forays into its neighbors' airspace. US F-15C Eagle pilots intercepted aircraft heading for NATO territory. After an exchange of hand signals, the Russians would turn for home, escorted by the Eagles.

EYEWITNESS

"I think the [CAP] mission is so important. The consequences of failing at this are large and very visible and deadly. That is the bottom line ... The longer we go between events, the more you have to work to keep yourself alert and make sure you are ready to go when the worst happens."

– CAP pilot, US Air Force

GLOSSARY

cockpit The part of an airplane where the pilot sits.

collateral damage Unintended damage to an area near a target.

dog-fight A one-on-one fight between fighter planes.

fuselage The body of an airplane.

infrared A kind of light wave that is not visible.

insurgents Rebels fighting against a government or an invasion force.

laser designator A laser beam used to pinpoint a target for a weapon.

Mach A unit for measuring speeds faster than the speed of sound.

morale The confidence a person or a group has in their own success.

ordnance Weapons such as bombs, rockets, or missiles.

pod A detachable unit full of specialist equipment.

radar A system that uses radio waves to detect objects.

reconnaissance Observation of an enemy's position.

simulator A machine that gives a realistic impression of how an airplane is controlled.

smart weapon A weapon that is guided to its target by computers.

sound barrier The speed at which an object equals the speed of sound, 1,122 feet per second (340.29 m/s).

stealth technology Technology used to disguise aircraft and vehicles to stop them being located by radar.

strafing When an airplane attacks a target repeatedly.

supersonic Describes something that travels faster than the speed of sound.

surveillance Close observation of the enemy.

turbo-prop A jet plane in which a turbine powers a propeller.

undercarriage The wheeled structure that supports an airplane.

FURTHER INFORMATION

BOOKS

Alpert, Barbera. *U.S. Military Fighter Planes*. U.S. Military Technology. North Mankato, MN: Capstone Press, 2012.

Corrigan, Jim. *Fighter Jets*. Military Experience in the Air. Greensboro, NC: Morgan Reynolds Publishing, 2013.

Gordon, Nick. *Fighter Pilot*. Torque Books. Minneapolis, MN: Bellwether Media, 2013.

Jackson, Robert. *101 Great Fighters*. 101 Greatest Weapons of All Times. New York: Rosen Publishing Group, 2015.

Loveless, Antony. *Fighter Pilots*. World's Most Dangerous Jobs. New York: Crabtree Publishing Company, 2009.

O'Grady, Scott, and Michael French. *Basher Five-Two*. New York: Yearling, 2010.

West, David, and James Field. *Fighter Pilots*. Graphic Careers. New York: Rosen Central, 2008.

WEBSITES

www.afrotc.com/college-life/flight
Introduction to a flight career from the Air Force ROTC (Reserve Officers' Training Corps).

www.usaf.com/1fight
Gallery of jet fighters in the US Air Force today.

usmilitary.about.com/of/airforcejoin/ss/afpilot.htm
Where to start if you want to become an Air Force pilot.

www.wikihow.com/Become-An-Air-Force-Pilot
Wikihow site about becoming a pilot, with a video.

Publisher's note to educators and parents: Our editors have carefully reviewed these websites to ensure that they are suitable for students. Many websites change frequently, however, and we cannot guarantee that a site's future contents will continue to meet our high standards of quality and educational value. Be advised that students should be closely supervised whenever they access the Internet.

INDEX